# Saint John Bosco
## and His

# BIG
# GRAY
# DOG

## Written and Illustrated by Hayley Medeiros
### CARITAS PRESS

# Saint John Bosco and His BIG GRAY DOG

**Saint John Bosco and His Big Gray Dog**
**Copyright © 2015 Hayley Medeiros**
**Printed in the USA**

First Edition
10 9 8 7 6 5 4 3 2 1
ISBN 978-1-940209-16-6

Contact Sherry@LilyTrilogy.com

# CARITAS PRESS

CaritasPress.org

For my mother,
whose faith in me
is unwavering

Once there lived a good man named John Bosco, who was born near Turin, Italy in 1815. From the time he was a small boy, John knew that he wanted to devote his life to doing the Lord's work. He became a kind and gentle priest, known for helping poor, homeless children who had nowhere to go and no one to love.

Good Father Bosco did more than feed, clothe, and house these poor children. He listened to their problems, comforted them, and taught them about their loving Father in heaven and how to live like Jesus.

Father Bosco went about his business doing the Lord's work. Believe it or not, there were people who didn't want him to help others. In fact, some people were so furious at Father Bosco's determination to continue his good work that they tried to hurt and even kill him. The good priest had to be very careful walking home alone, especially after dark.

Late one night as Father Bosco made his way back home to the Oratory, the home he founded for poor and abandoned children, he felt terribly afraid. Suddenly, a huge, wolf-like dog with gray fur appeared out of nowhere and walked beside him until he reached his home. The good priest named his new friend Grigio, which means "Gray One" in Italian. This was the first of many times that Grigio escorted Father Bosco home before disappearing alone into the woods.

One foggy November evening, good Father Bosco was returning home after working in the slums of Turin during the day. Suddenly, he noticed two men following him. Father Bosco tried to cross the street and turn around to go the other way, but it was too late. The men jumped the good priest from behind and flung a large cloak over his head. Father Bosco tried to shout for help, but his muffled cries could barely be heard.

Out of thin air, Grigio appeared. Baring his large teeth, he growled fiercely at the men before leaping up and lunging at them in a vicious attack.

"Call off your dog!" one of the attackers shouted.

"I'll call him off only if you promise never to attack another passerby," Father Bosco answered calmly.

"Call him off NOW!" the other attacker screamed, as Grigio lunged.

"Grigio, my friend, be still," soothed Father Bosco. Grigio continued to growl and bare his teeth so menacingly that the two attackers beat a path into the woods as fast as their legs could carry them.

Good Father Bosco breathed a huge sigh of relief. "Thank you, my Grigio," the priest said affectionately, as he hugged and patted his protector. "You are truly a gift from God!"

As if Grigio could understand and wanted to say "you're welcome," he jumped up on Father Bosco and began to lick the priest's face, wagging his tail in glee. Father Bosco went home that night accompanied yet again by his faithful canine friend.

Grigio became known to all of the children at the Oratory as Father Bosco's dog. Some children and even adults were frightened when they saw the fearsome-looking animal appear for a visit. "Do not be afraid," Father Bosco would say. "It is only my Grigio coming to say hello. Let him come to me." The children would pat and stroke Grigio's beautiful gray fur and then bring him to the priest wherever he happened to be.

Life continued in this way for years until finally, Grigio seemed to have disappeared for good.

Over ten years later, Father Bosco was traveling on foot to visit some friends at their farmhouse far outside the city of Milan. The journey took longer than he expected. As the skies darkened after dusk, the good priest began to fear once more for his safety. "Oh, if only I had my Grigio, how fortunate I would be!" the priest thought sadly to himself.

As if the mere thought had summoned him, Grigio appeared out of nowhere, whimpering joyfully and wagging his tail. He was thrilled to see his good friend Father Bosco again. Just as he had done many times before, Grigio accompanied the priest the final two miles until he reached his destination.

Good Father Bosco sat down to the evening meal in the company of his friends in their cozy farmhouse, while Grigio napped peacefully nearby.

At the end of the meal, Father Bosco's friend prepared a bowl of pasta to bring to Grigio, but when the man looked for the dog, he was gone. Father Bosco and the entire family searched high and low for Grigio, but he had truly vanished. Although this surprised his friends, it did not surprise the good priest. In all the years that Grigio appeared to help Father Bosco, he was never known to eat or drink.

This was by far not the last time that Grigio appeared to Father Bosco and others.

How can we explain the amazing Grigio, who appeared just when he was needed most? How can we explain how he appeared and disappeared in different places over the course of more than thirty years? Surely God must have sent an angel in the form of a big gray dog to protect and befriend Father Bosco, so he could continue to do the Lord's work.

Isn't there a little bit of Grigio in all of our beloved, faithful animal companions? After all, our loving pets are a wonderful gift given to us by our loving, caring Father in heaven.

# Afterword

Even among saints, the life of Giovanni Melchiorre Bosco (1815-1888) is considered remarkable for its numerous supernatural and miraculous occurrences. He was affectionately known as "Don" (Father) Bosco to his Italian countrymen. The story of Grigio is historically documented in many sources, not the least of them Don Bosco's own autobiography, *Memoirs of the Oratory of Saint Francis de Sales*. In fact, he entitled the final chapter of his memoir "Grigio." *Saint John Bosco and His Big Gray Dog* is based on the primary source of Don Bosco's memoir, not on the plentiful tales of Grigio told by Bosco's many biographers, friends, and acquaintances. Many people saw Grigio on multiple occasions from about 1852 until approximately 1883. However, the saint himself only wrote about the episodes covered in this book. The Salesian sisters claimed to have experienced Grigio's protection on three occasions between 1898 and 1930 as well.

Don Bosco endured great persecution at the hands of people who were anti-Catholic. Priests were the very symbol of the Church they hated, and they wanted to put an end to Don Bosco's good work with poor and abandoned children.

During Giovanni Bosco's lifetime, Grigio was the topic of much debate and speculation among those who knew him for his role as the priest's guardian and companion. Don Bosco tried several times to learn where the dog came from, but in the end, he simply accepted Grigio as a gift from God. "What does it matter?" he wrote. "What counts is that he was my friend. I only know that the animal was truly providential for me on many occasions when I found myself in danger." In *Secrets of the Saints*, French Catholic author Henri Ghéon writes, "An angel could quite well take the form of a dog. At the very least, we can assert that the animal—if animal it was—had a nose for sanctity and would fight for it. If it was a miracle, God worked so many other miracles for Don Bosco that this one need not surprise us." Angel or miracle? You be the judge.

What is certain, however, is that in the life of Giovanni Bosco, the extraordinary was the ordinary. The story of Don Bosco and Grigio not only has much to teach us about unconditional love and friendship, but it also shows us how God will give us the help we need in order to carry out His work on earth.

Photo By Fontevrault (Own work)
[Public domain], via Wikimedia Commons

## ABOUT CARITAS PRESS

Caritas Press was founded in 2011 with the mission of shedding light on things eternal in a culture that is becoming increasingly blind to the wonders of God's works and numb to His boundless love. Making use of the subtle and the beautiful, Caritas Press hopes to play a part in igniting in children and adults a desire to know God more fully. For a full listing of all Caritas titles for children, youths and adults, visit CaritasPress.org.

CaritasPress.org

**Miraculous Me**
*Ruth Pendergast Sissel and Tina Tolliver Matney*

**Barnyard Bliss**
*Ruth Pendergast Sissel and Tina Tolliver Matney*

**Victoria's Sparrows** *by Sherry Boas*

**Little Maximus Myers** *by Sherry Boas*

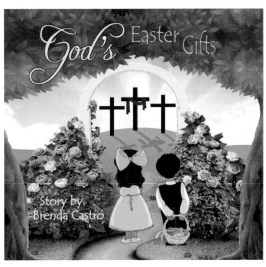

**God's Easter Gifts** *by Brenda Castro*

**Billowtail:
A Novel**
*by Sherry Boas*

Made in the USA
Monee, IL
02 January 2025

75879239R00021